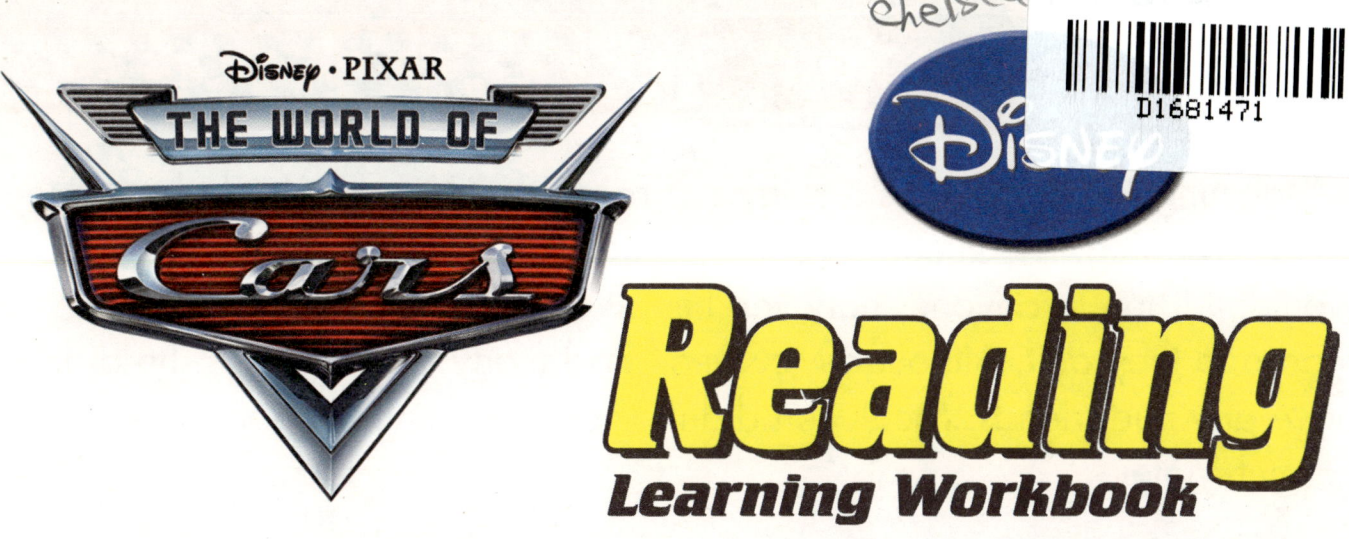

Reading
Learning Workbook

- **Reading Comprehension**
- **Basic Reading Skills**
- **Engaging Activities**

Bendon Publishing International, Inc.
Ashland, OH 44805
www.bendonpub.com

Copyright © 2008 Disney Enterprises, Inc./Pixar
Disney/Pixar elements; ©Disney/Pixar; Hudson Hornet is a trademark of DaimlerChrysler; Fiat is a trademark of Fiat S.p.A.; Mack is a registered trademark of Mack Trucks, Inc.; Chevrolet Impala is a trademark of General Motors; Porsche is a trademark of Porsche; Plymouth Superbird is a trademark of DaimlerChrysler; Ferrari elements are trademarks of Ferrari S.p.A.; Petty marks used by permission of Petty Marketing LLC.

Comprehension

Lightning McQueen was a shiny red race car. He only cared about one thing—winning. McQueen thought he could do <u>everything himself</u>. He wouldn't listen to <u>anyone</u>, not even his pit crew. This made his pit crew mad and they quit. Although McQueen had many adoring fans, he didn't have any true friends. McQueen didn't know how to be a good friend until he met Mater.

What Did You Learn?
Using the story as a guide, write 3 facts about McQueen below:

1. He was a shiny red race car.
2. He liked to race and winning
3. He met Mater, a new friend.

Deductive Thinking

Follow the directions below to color the scene from the Piston Cup.

Color the first car red.

The last car is yellow.

The green car is directly in front of the yellow car.

The blue car is behind the red car.

Where is the purple car?

Story Sequence

The race for the Piston Cup was about to begin. Lightning McQueen pulled out of his Rust-eze trailer. "I'm faster than fast, and quicker than quick," he said. "I am SPEED! Ka-Chow!!" The hot shot race car turned to the side, showing off his lightning bolt. McQueen wanted to win the Piston Cup and the Dinoco sponsorship. Chick Hicks, The King, and McQueen pulled up to the starting line. The fans cheered as the race began!

Story Sequence
Using the story as a guide, put the sentences below in the correct order.

_____   McQueen said, "I am SPEED! Ka-chow!!"

_____   The fans cheered as the race began!

_____   Chick Hicks, The King and McQueen pulled up to the starting line.

_____   Lightning McQueen pulled out of his Rust-eze trailer.

Recall 3-2-1
Name the 3 cars that were racing?

_____ , _____ , and _____

McQueen wanted to win what 2 things?

_____ and _____

What was 1 thing Lightning McQueen said?

_____

What did you learn?

Using the story from the previous page, answer the question below. Then, unscramble the letters to check your answer. **iPtosnpCu**
Lightning McQueen, The King, and Chick Hicks were in a race for the

_____.

Question words (who, what, why, where, when, and how) are often used to help us remember what we read. Use the questions below to see how much you remember. Read the story again if necessary.

WHO was Lightning McQueen racing against?

_____

WHAT did McQueen say as he pulled out of his trailer?

_____

WHERE did the cars line up?

_____

WHEN did the fans cheer?

_____

WHY did McQueen want to win the race?

_____

HOW did McQueen show off his lightning bolt?

_____

Word Recognition

Lightning McQueen was a very fast race car. He was so fast that he did not think he needed help from anyone. During the race for the Piston Cup, McQueen refused to stop to have his tires changed. As a result, McQueen's tire popped on the last lap of the race. McQueen lost control of his car and nearly lost the race.

Word Recognition

Circle the word "race" every time it appears in the story.
How many times did the word "race" appear? _____

Story Sequence

Using the story as a guide, put the sentences below in the correct order.

_____ McQueen popped his tire.

_____ McQueen did not think he needed any help.

_____ Lightning McQueen lost control.

_____ McQueen would not stop to have his tired changed.

Look, Read, Think

Sometimes we use pictures to help us understand what we are reading. Look at each picture. Then, read the sentences to the right. Mark the sentence that describes each picture.

3/3

☐ Luigi is wearing a blue hat.

☑ Luigi is waving two flags.

☐ Luigi is a green car.

☐ Red is squirting water on a fire.

☐ Red is a big, red race car.

☑ Red is watering a flower.

☑ Guido is lifting four tires.

☐ Guido is a tow truck.

☐ Guido is changing a tire.

7

Mar 9, 2010

Context Clues

A good reader uses clues from a sentence and pictures to determine the meaning of unfamiliar words. Fill in the missing words in the story below by using clues from the sentence, word bank, and picture.

finish
California
announcer
results

impossible
Dinoco
tie
Chick

"Down the stretch they come!" shouted the _____. The King and _____ were catching up to McQueen. As they crossed the finish line, it was _____ to tell who had won. McQueen was sure that the Piston Cup would be his. The _____ were announced. It was a three-way tie! The tie-breaker race would be held in _____ in one week. McQueen did not have time to talk to anyone. He had to be the first to get to California and the _____ team.

You're Invited!

What: Piston Cup Tiebreaker Race
Where: California
When: One week from today
Why: To cheer on the teams as they race for the Piston Cup.

Read the invitation. Write the correct answer on the line.

1. The race is for _____

2. When is the race? _____

3. Where will the race take place? _____

4. Why have you been invited? _____

Reader Recall

While heading for the big race, McQueen got lost. He looked everywhere for Mack but could not find him. In the middle of the dessert, all alone, McQueen began to get scared. Panicked, he started to drive faster. Out of nowhere, Sheriff turned on his lights and began to race after McQueen. McQueen kept driving. He ran into fences and tore up the road. When the chase ended, Sheriff took McQueen to jail. McQueen was in a lot of trouble!

Reader Recall

The main idea is what the story or paragraph is all about. It is the most important idea in a paragraph. What is the main idea of the paragraph above? Use 15 words or less.

_____   _____   _____
_____   _____   _____
_____   _____   _____
_____   _____   _____
_____   _____   _____

Reader Retell

It is important to recognize the beginning, middle, and end of a story. In your own words, briefly rewrite the beginning, middle, and end of the story from the previous page.

Beginning: _____

_____

_____

Middle: _____

_____

_____

End: _____

_____

_____

Reader Recall

Doc wanted McQueen to leave Radiator Springs right away. Doc thought that McQueen had done enough damage already. Plus, Doc really didn't like race cars. But Sally and the other cars thought that McQueen should fix the road before he could leave. Doc agreed to the deal. McQueen began to work on the road right away. However, McQueen was in such a rush to get to his race that he made the road a bumpy mess! Doc was very mad. He challenged McQueen to a race. "If you win," said Doc, "you are free to go. But if I win, you will stay until the road is fixed right." McQueen agreed to the deal. It seemed like an easy win to McQueen. What McQueen didn't know was that Doc used to be a race car himself!

Reader Recall

Which of the following is true?
  a. Doc let McQueen go.
  b. Sally thought McQueen should work at the Cozy Cone Motel to pay for the damage.
  c. The town decided that McQueen should fix the road before he could leave.
  d. Doc told McQueen he could fix the road after his race in California.

Predicting

A **prediction** is what you think will happen. A prediction is similar to a guess. We use facts from a story to support our predictions.

In Your Own Words
Use the story from the previous page. Predict what will happen next. Remember, a prediction is what you think will happen.

_____
_____
_____

What makes you think this will happen? Use support (facts) from the reading.

_____
_____
_____

Reader Recall

Doc Hudson used to be a famous race car, but was forced to leave the racing world after a bad crash. Doc moved to Radiator Springs and became the judge and doctor of the small, quiet town. All was calm in the town until the day McQueen arrived. Doc did not like McQueen at first because he thought McQueen was selfish and rude. After spending some time in Radiator Springs, McQueen began to change. As a result, Doc's feelings toward McQueen began to change as well.

Reader Recall

1. What was Doc before he moved to Radiator Springs?
   a. teacher   b. race car   c. lawyer   d. sheriff

2. Why was Doc forced to leave that job?
   a. He had a bad bad crash.
   b. He was too old.
   c. He cheated.
   d. He was rude.

3. Doc was the _____ of Radiator Springs.
   a. sheriff   b. judge   c. nurse   d. mechanic

4. Did Doc's feelings toward McQueen change?
   Yes   No

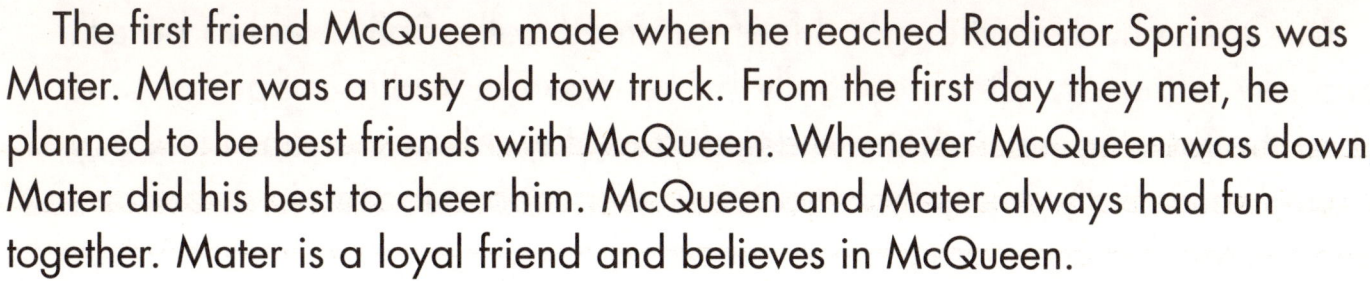
Character Chart

The first friend McQueen made when he reached Radiator Springs was Mater. Mater was a rusty old tow truck. From the first day they met, he planned to be best friends with McQueen. Whenever McQueen was down, Mater did his best to cheer him. McQueen and Mater always had fun together. Mater is a loyal friend and believes in McQueen.

Complete the character map for Mater below. Use the paragraph above to fill in each space.

Appearance
What did Mater look like?

Character
Mater

Feelings
How did Mater feel about McQueen?

Actions
What did Mater do?

Reader Recall

McQueen had another good friend named Sally. Sally used to be an attorney in the city. One day, Sally broke down in Radiator Springs. She liked the town so much that she decided to stay. Now she runs the Cozy Cone Motel. Sally hopes that McQueen will choose to stay in Radiator Springs too.

Recall 3-2-1

What 3 things did you learn about Sally?

1. _____
2. _____
3. _____

What 2 jobs has Sally had?

1. _____
2. _____

What is 1 reason that Sally might want McQueen to stay in Radiator Springs?

_____
_____

Reader Recall

Radiator Springs is a small town in Carburetor County. When McQueen reached Radiator Springs, the town was run down. Radiator Springs used to be full of life, but travelers no longer stopped on their way through. Many visitors now bypassed Radiator Springs by traveling on Route 66. Route 66 was a big road that allowed travelers to get where they were going faster. McQueen believed that with a little help, Radiator Springs could be beautiful again.

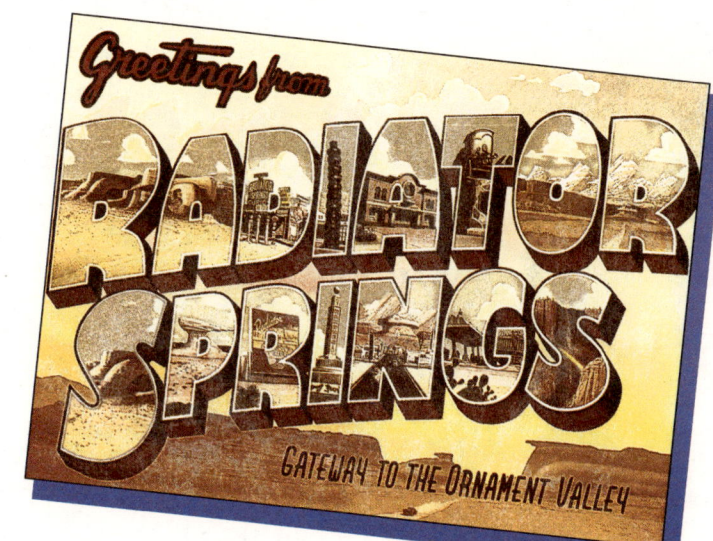

Reader Recall

Radiator Springs is a small town in what county?

_____

Why did travelers no longer stop in Radiator Springs?

_____

_____

What did McQueen believe that Radiator Springs could be?

_____

_____

What is Route 66?

_____

17

Setting Mural

The **setting** is where and when a story takes place. Create a setting mural in the space below by drawing a picture of Radiator Springs.

RADIATOR SPRINGS

Main Idea Match

There is one sentence in each paragraph below that does not "fit" or belong. Underline the sentence that should be removed from each paragraph.

Mater and McQueen always had fun together. Sally was a good friend too. When McQueen was sad, Mater did his best to cheer him. Mater taught McQueen how to drive backwards and tip tractors. Above all, Mater taught McQueen how to be a good friend.

McQueen used to think that winning was everything. After spending some time in Radiator Springs, he began to change his mind. No one could find Lightning McQueen. When McQueen finally slowed down, he made many friends. McQueen realized that winning races wasn't as important as being respectful and having great friends.

Story Sequence

Pictures can also be used to tell a story. Finish drawing pictures in the boxes below to tell your own story about McQueen and his friends.

Cause and Effect

Cause and effect is when one event leads to another.

The **cause** is why something happens. Ask yourself, "Why did it happen?"

The **effect** is what happens as a result. Ask yourself, "What happened?"

For example: The boy hit a home run. The fans cheered.

The **cause** is the boy hitting the home run.

The **effect** is that the fans cheered.

McQueen kept his promise and finished the road. Now, he could leave for California, but McQueen wasn't as excited as he thought he would be. McQueen had made so many great friends; he was sad to leave. McQueen's new friends in Radiator Springs were sad too. McQueen finally knew that there were more important things than racing.

Using the paragraph above as a guide, complete the table below. The first one is done as an example for you to follow.

CAUSE	EFFECT
The boy hit a home run.	The fans cheered.
McQueen finished the road.	
	McQueen was sad to leave.

Story Sequence

Read the paragraph below. Then, use the story as a guide to mark McQueen's route on the map below.

Before McQueen left for California, there were a few things he still had to do. McQueen wanted to thank his new friends. He fixed up their shops so they looked new again. McQueen also had to get himself fixed up. First, Red washed McQueen. Then, Luigi and Guido gave him their best set of white-wall tires. Finally, Ramone gave him a fancy new paint job. McQueen was ready to surprise his friends with his new look and the new look of Radiator Springs!

Picture Clues

Circle the correct answer. Use the picture as a guide.

1. Lightning McQueen is red.

    YES   NO

2. His lightning bolt is green.

    YES   NO

3. McQueen is number 95.

    YES   NO

4. McQueen has white-wall tires.

    YES   NO

5. The Rust-Eze logo is on the car

    YES   NO

6. McQueen's tires say "LIGHTYEAR."

    YES   NO

23

Reader Recall

McQueen arrived at the Piston Cup to find that he had a new pit crew led by Doc! McQueen didn't win the Piston Cup because he now knew that helping a friend was more important. As McQueen pushed The King across the finish line, he smiled. Finally, McQueen realized that winning wasn't everything. In fact, it was much more important to be a good friend!

Reader Recall

During the big race, McQueen helped _____.

    a. Mater   b. Chick Hicks   c. The King   d. Doc

Who belonged to McQueen's pit crew?

    a. Tia and Mia

    b. His new friends

    c. The old Rust-Eze pit crew

    d. Dinoco's pit crew

Main Idea

What is the main idea of the paragraph on the previous page?

a. Being a good friend is more important than winning

b. Sally and McQueen were best friends

c. Doc was McQueen's crew chief

Reader Response

1. Did McQueen eventually like Radiator Springs?   YES   NO

2. What makes you think this way? Use support from the text.

_____

_____

3. Have you ever disliked something at first and then later changed your mind? Write a few sentences about an experience you had that was similar to McQueen's.

_____

_____

Compare & Contrast

Sometimes it is useful to find similarities and differences between characters in a story. Complete the chart below by filling in traits for each character. Then, circle any traits that are the same between the two. Write the circled traits on the list labeled "Alike." The first one is done for you.

Lightning McQueen — **Alike** — **Doc**

Lightning McQueen	Alike	Doc
Red		Blue
(Car)	Car	(Car)

Fact and Opinion

A statement of **fact** can be proven true or false. An **opinion** tells what one person thinks, feels, or believes. It cannot be proven.

Read the sentences below. Underline each statement of fact. Circle each statement that is an opinion.

Radiator Springs is a great place to live.

Sally runs the Cozy Cone Motel.

Travelers bypassed Radiator Springs by driving on Route 66.

Tractor tipping is fun.

Mater liked McQueen right away.

Being the sheriff of Radiator Springs is a great job.

Story Map

Using a combination of the stories throughout this workbook, complete the story map below. For some sections you may have more than one answer.

The Setting	**The Characters**
The Problem	**The Solution**